Hope: A poem book about life

Angela Munoz-Pacheco

Presentation by *BookLeaf Publishing*

Web: www.bookleafpub.com

E-mail: info@bookleafpub.com

ISBN: 9789358316179

First edition 2023

DEDICATION

Dedicated to my mom Judith who has always been there for me no matter how many mistakes I make and to my sister who is always making me laugh even through our silly fights.

ACKNOWLEDGEMENT

I would like to acknowledge my mom who has always been there through thick and thin no matter what I do or how many mistakes I make I can always count on her.

PREFACE

Some poems will make you cry, some will make you laugh, some will make you think about what is going on in the world around us.

A Mom

A mom is like an owl beautiful and wise
Someone you can be yourself with
A mom is someone who can make your heart
Beat a million times a minute
A mom is like a sunflower
Standing straight, tall and proud
A mom is someone you can look up to
A mom is someone who will always be proud
Of your accomplishments
A mom is like a star always shining bright
Always there for you, shining for you
No matter where you go
A mom's arms are the best place to be
As she hugs you tight
For we would not be in this world
If we did not have a mom.

Sister

I know I never tell you
this
You are one of the best
things
That has happened in my
life
We have fought, laughed,
Played and cried
You are not only my sister
But also a friend
We may not always show our love
But I know we still love each other
No matter what, even though
We may sometimes drive each other crazy
But what else are sisters for
I will always be here for you
Through thick and thin
As you have always been for me
Through all the memories we share
Sharing the good times and the bad times
No matter, there has always been love
Though not always visible
I am glad God placed you in my path
I am proud and blessed
To call you my sister

Miss you

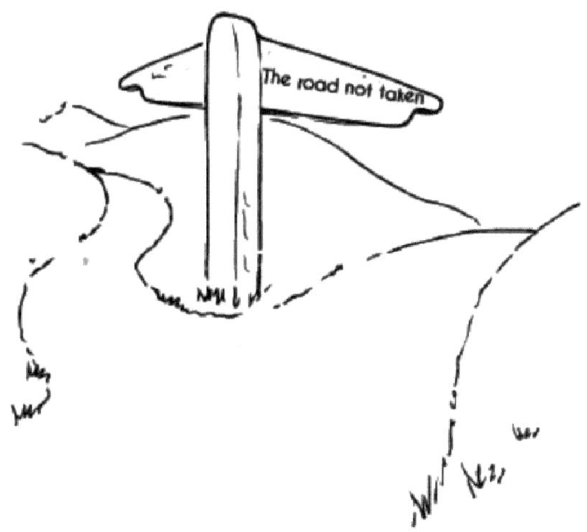

You were here for so long
Yet the short time I knew you
You stole my heart
I know it hurt you
It hurt me too
But now that you are gone
All I know is I miss you
I know I am not perfect
I know I will never be
I just hope you are up there
Proud of me
I thought you had more time
Here on earth

I know you had to let go
Even though you were
Holding on for so long
I now know you are
No longer in pain
For you are free
There is not a day that goes by
Where I do not think of you
All promises we made
I am still trying to keep
I might be selfish
But oh how I wish
You could have stayed longer
I want you to know
You will always be in my heart
I will always be thinking of you
As I miss you, oh so much
Everyday of my life
Till we see each other once again

No matter

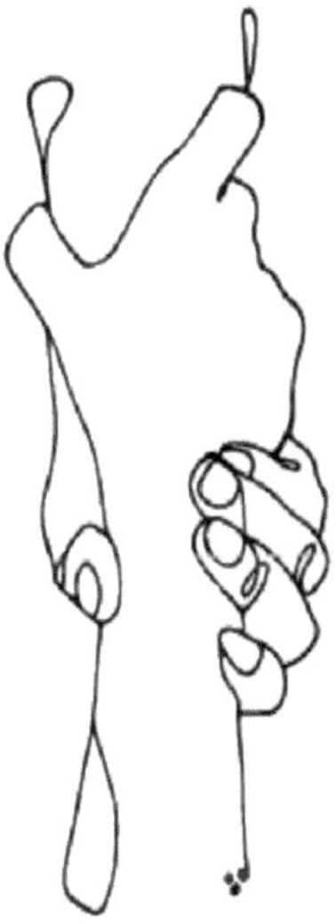

No matter where I go
I always see your smiling
face
When I feel sad or mad
You are always there
cheering me up making me
laugh
From the first time we met
Doing races to get things
done
Made it way more fun
Than if I were to do it on
my own
No matter what happens
You have always been there for me
From the good times to the bad
I will also always be here for you
No matter what
From the stormy nights,
You are the ray of sunshine
Sneaking out from behind those clouds
No matter what
I will always be here for you
As you have always been for me

Christmas is coming

Christmas time is coming
Time for getting out the
Tape and scissors
To wrap the presents
Every time I put those
Two together
They seem to wander off
Now where did I put them
Are they on the floor
Or under the paper
Keep on searching
Maybe I need to call
In the rescue squad
Search up high
Search down low
Over the river

Through the woods
Here we go
Oh wait they were in
My pocket this whole time.
Set them on the table
Now to finish wrapping
Reaching for tape and scissors
Now here we go again
Now where did they go

Butterflies

Butterflies flutter, delicate and light,
Painting the air with hues so bright.
They dance on the breeze, graceful and free,
A waltz of wings, a sight to see.

Their fragile beauty, a fragile disguise,
A symbol of change, of life's surprise.
From humble cocoons, they emerge anew,
Transformed, reborn, in colors that imbue.

From garden to meadow, they gracefully roam,
Seeking nectar, finding their own home.
They flutter and flit, a whimsical display,

A reminder to live, to seize the day.

Their delicate wings, a language unspoken,
Whispering secrets, stories unbroken.
They teach us to embrace life's fleeting grace,
To embrace the unknown, to find our own space.

Butterflies, enchanting creatures of flight,
Remind us to follow our dreams, to take flight.
In their presence, we find solace and peace,
As we watch them soar, our worries release.

So let us be like butterflies, gentle and free,
Embracing change, embracing what could be.
For in their flight, we find inspiration,
To live with purpose, with determination.

Butterflies, oh how you captivate,
With your delicate beauty, you fascinate.
May we learn from you, and never forget,
To let our spirits soar, with no regrets.

Be you

In the vast expanse of dreams untold,
Where limitless possibilities unfold,
There lies a spirit, strong and bold,
A beacon of light, a story to be told.

Oh, to be the best you can be,
To set the world ablaze with fire,
With unwavering determination, higher,
A force unyielding, a soul on fire.

No obstacles, no barriers, can confine you,
The boundless potential within your mind,
For in this realm, dreams intertwine,
As the spirit soars, transcending time.

Let not the whispers of doubt prevail,
Nor the cynics' words that make you fail,
For you possess a strength beyond
What you know,
A resilience that will always prevail.

Embrace the challenges, embrace the fights,
Ignite the passion that burns so bright,
For in your heart, the spark takes flight,
And you'll conquer mountains with all your
might.

No dream too grand, no goal too vast,
When you believe in yourself,
you're unsurpassed,
With every step, the die is cast,
A legacy forged, destined to last.

So, let the doubters fade away,
As you march forward, come what may,
With every stride, you'll pave the way,
Proven them wrong
To a brighter future, where dreams hold sway.

In this tapestry of life, you're the weaver,
The architect of dreams, a true believer,
With courage as your sword, your shield,
You'll conquer all, never to yield.

For you are capable of anything, truly,
A force of nature, fierce and unruly,
So let your spirit soar, wild and free,
And become the best version of you.

Hope

Glimmer in twilight,
Hope's gentle flame flickers bright,
Like a candle burning
Guiding you through the night.

In the darkest hour,
Hope whispers, "I will be there,"

Lifting burdens bare

Through trials and strife,
Hope breathes new meaning to life,
Bringing healing rife.

Like a blooming bud,
Hope spreads its wings, soaring free,
Embracing all we see.

With each sunrise's gleam,
Hope paints dreams on life's wide seam,
Igniting endless beam.

In the depths of gloom,
Hope blossoms, dispelling doom,
Revealing a bloom.
Hope's song softly sings,
Melodies of what could be,
Inspiring our wings.

In fragile embrace,
Hope weaves a tapestry grand,
Binding heart and hand.

Though shadows may creep,
Hope's light will forever keep,
Faith alive, not sleep.

Through every trial,
Hope stands tall, unwavering,
Ever so versatile.

In each fleeting breath,
Hope carries us through life's test,
Leaving doubt bereft.

In the face of fear,
Hope's resilience will appear,
Whispering, "Draw near."

With each passing day,
Hope's flame burns brighter, they say,
Lighting our own way.

So let hope ignite,
Fill your heart with radiant light,
Guiding you aright.

Counting

One, two, three, four boom
one two three four boom
I keep on counting
repeating to four
calming down as
it gets louder
trying to drown out the noise of the storm
one two three the shorter the counting
the further the storm gets
it's okay to be scared
just keep on counting
one two boom
storm is starting to disappear
and the night seems to get quieter
one boom soon there's no more flashes of
lighting or thunder sounds
there is just silence

Teaching

Tiny minds eager,
Learning and growing each day,
Guiding their bright way.

Colors and numbers,
Letters and rhymes fill their world,
Knowledge unfurled.

Patience and kindness,
Nurturing hearts and spirits,
Teaching little souls.

Inquisitive eyes,
Curiosity abounds,
Wonders to be found.

Gentle hands guiding,

As they grasp life's mysteries,
Tiny victories.

Teachers, light the path,
Ignite the flame of learning,
Forever impart.

Children's Innocence

In a world where children play and dance
In laughter's joy, where innocence resides,
Where children dance and play in mirthful chase,
A realm of wonders, where delight presides,
Their gleeful souls, a testament of grace.

With giggles pure, their laughter fills the air,
Like tinkling bells that echo through the trees,
Their hearts unburdened, free from worldly care,
They find in play the joys that truly please.

Their tiny hands hold treasures yet unknown,
Imagination guides their every move,
In make-believe, a kingdom they have grown,
Where dreams take flight and magic does exist

Children blessed with hearts so light,
Their laughter brings such beauty to our sight.

Innocence, their armor, shields their soul,
From life's harsh knocks and bitter wounds it keeps,
Their spirits soar, untouched by sorrow's toll,
As laughter dances on their rosy cheeks.
Oh, how they revel in the simplest things,
A silly joke, a tickle's gentle touch,
Their laughter like a symphony that sings,
A melody of innocence and such.

In games they find a world of endless fun,
With boundless energy, they run and play,
Never getting tired
Their laughter, like a race that's just begun,
Brings sunshine to the darkest of each day.

Their laughter, like a potion, heals the heart,
Dispelling sadness with its vibrant hue,
In every giggle, troubles do depart,
Revealing life's pure essence, ever true.

Oh, children laughing, funny and so bright,
In your sweet innocence, we find delight.

Their playful innocence, a wondrous sight,

As laughter weaves its magic through their days
and nights,
With every giggle, darkness turns to light,
And sorrows fade like morning mist ablaze.

Their laughter, like a fountain, ever flows,
Refreshing spirits weary from the fight,
With every chuckle, happiness it shows,
A beacon shining in the darkest night.
Like a candle burning bright

Let us cherish their infectious glee,
For in their laughter, love and
hope reside in them
Their funny antics bring us to our knees,
Making us laugh and giggle
As joy within our hearts becomes their guide.

Children, laughing, playing with such grace,
In your pure innocence, we will find our place.

Peace

There is war going on left and right
People arguing on where to stand
Innocent lives are being taken
Can we just not have peace
Stop with the fighting
Can you not see

Instead of living in the future
Moving forward in time
We are going back
History is repeating

Let the war stop
As children are dying
Some who barely
have had a chance to live
To be a child
Do you not want
A world with no war
A world where we all
Can get along and have
A world where we have peace

Silly Parakeet (Poem about a parakeet named Cookie)

Silly parakeet,
Repeating everything we say
Colors bright, feathers so neat,
Chirping in delight.

Wings spread, he takes flight,
Dancing in the morning light,
Joyful, such a sight.

Our Mom

In the stillness of a morning's embrace,
A presence so ethereal, with gentle grace,
She breathes life into the world, every day anew,
A beacon of love, a bond forever true.

Unseen hands that guide, comfort, and heal,

Her touch, a balm, to every wound she seals,
With eyes that hold stories, both joy and pain,
She weaves a tapestry of love, again and again.

Her voice, a lullaby, a symphony of care,
Whispering secrets, melodies rare,
She sings of dreams, of hope and might,
Igniting flames within, a guiding light.

A warrior, fierce, both tender and strong,
She battles for her kin, against all wrong,
Her shield of courage, her heart pure and kind,
A fortress of love, forever intertwined.

Through sleepless nights and endless chores,
She gives her all, and then gives more,
Her selflessness, a testament to her worth,
A living testament, the essence of birth.

In her embrace, we find solace and peace,
A sanctuary of love, where worries cease,
She nurtures our souls, like a garden in bloom,
A bouquet of memories, forever in bloom.

Through trials and triumphs, she'll always be there,
A constant companion, a love beyond compare,
For she is our anchor, our guiding star,
Our mom, our rock, no matter how far.

So let us celebrate this beacon of light,
With gratitude and love, shining ever so bright,
For she is the heartbeat, the very core,
Our mom, our muse, forevermore.

Rainy Day

On a rainy cloudy day, darkness looms overhead,
A symphony of raindrops, a somber tune is spread.
The sky adorned in shades of gray, a melancholy sight,
But hidden within the storm, a seed of hope takes flight.

The clouds weep tears from heaven, as if to cleanse the earth,
Drenching every blade of grass, giving life its rebirth.
Each droplet a precious jewel, glistening upon the leaves,
Nature's tears of sorrow, a balm for wounds it conceives.

Yet amidst the dreary downpour, a glimmer starts to rise,
A subtle shift in the atmosphere, a break within the skies.
A ray of golden sunlight pierces through the gray expanse,
Painting vibrant hues upon the world, a rainbow's joyful dance.

Oh, the beauty that emerges after the storm has passed,
As if the heavens wept their tears and made a pact at last.
A tapestry of colors, a promise in the air,
That after every tempest, there's a moment sweet and rare.

The rainbows arch across the heavens, like a bridge to dreams,

A reminder that even in darkness, hope's eternal gleam.
The storm may rage and thunder, but it cannot endure,
For sunshine waits beyond the clouds, steadfast and pure.

So let the rain pour endlessly, let the clouds fill the sky,
For in the midst of life's storms, we learn to truly fly.
And when the day is darkest, and hope seems far away,
Remember the rainbows that follow, after the storm's dismay.

A Bond

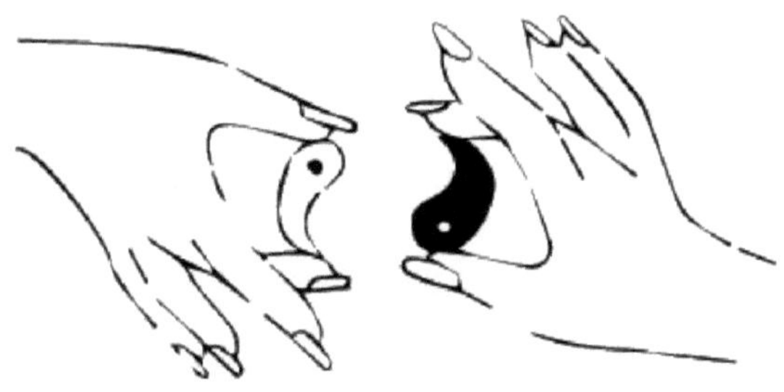

Sister, a bond beyond blood and birth,
A connection sewn deep in the fabric of our existence,
For you, I pen these words, a tribute to your worth.

In childhood days, we played and laughed,
Exploring the world, hand in hand,
Through fields of wildflowers, our spirits danced,
Imagining a future, where dreams would expand.

As time slipped by, our paths diverged,
Yet, the ties that bound us remained unbroken,
Through life's trials and triumphs we surged,
Our sisterhood, a steadfast token.

In moments of darkness, you were my light,
A beacon of hope, a shelter from the storm,
Your love, a balm that healed my plight,
Embracing me, making me feel reborn.

Through whispered secrets and shared dreams,
We forged a bond that would withstand,
The passage of time, the ebb and flow of streams,
A connection that transcended the mundane.

You are my confidante, my rock, my guide,
In you, I find solace, acceptance, and trust,
Through laughter and tears, side by side,
Together, we've weathered life's unjust.

Oh, sister, how grateful I am for your embrace,
For the way you've shaped me, made me whole,
In your presence, I find comfort and grace,
A kindred spirit, etched deep within my soul.

So, let these verses serve as a testament,
To the bond we share, so rare and true,
May our sisterhood forever be eminent,
A treasure I hold dear, forever anew.

Laughs and Giggles

Funny laughter rings,
Silly antics bring delight,
Happiness springs.

Giggles fill the air,
Silliness takes us away,
Laughter we all share.

Tickles and jokes told,
Mirth and joy intertwining,
Smiles never fold.

Silly faces make,
Laughter dances in our eyes,
Happiness awake.

In silly moments,
We find joy and pure delight,
Laughter's sweet scents.

Funny, happy, free,
Silliness sets our hearts free,
Laughter's melody.

In this world so vast,
Being silly is the key,
To happiness, fast.

So let's embrace fun,
Be silly, laugh and enjoy,
Our joy, never done.

Eternal Connection

Sometimes, when the world grows quiet,
And the weight of loneliness settles in,
The only solace I seek is in heaven,
Where my best friend now resides.

Oh, how I long for our conversations,
The laughter that filled our souls,
But now, the emptiness echoes,
For you are no longer here to hold.

In moments of joy or sorrow,
When the world feels too much to bear,
I yearn for your gentle presence,
To listen, to understand, to care.

I search for signs in the starry night,
In the whispers of the morning breeze,
Hoping to feel your loving essence,
To find comfort and be at ease.

But sometimes, my dear friend,
The distance feels immeasurable,
And the ache of missing you intensifies,
Leaving my heart irreparably vulnerable.

Yet, I find solace in the belief,
That though you are physically gone,
Our bond remains unbreakable,
In the realm where spirits are drawn.

So, I'll send my thoughts to the heavens,
Whispering secrets only we share,
Knowing that, in some ethereal way,

You are listening, you are there.

For in the silence, I'll find strength,
To navigate this world without you,
And cherish the memories we created,
Until we reunite in the skies so blue.

Until that day, my dear best friend,
I'll hold you close in my heart,
Finding solace in our eternal connection,
Even though we're worlds apart.

Be Kind

In this vast world, so full of faces unknown,
Where hearts hide stories yet to be shown,
Let us remember, in each fleeting encounter,
To be kind, for we know not what lies under.

Be kind to one another, with open hearts,
For we carry burdens, invisible parts,
Sorrows hidden beneath smiles we wear,
Struggles, battles fought, in quiet despair.

A gentle word, a touch of empathy's grace,
Can mend wounds unseen, bring solace,
embrace,

For every soul carries its own private storm,
A tempest of emotions, fragile and worn.

Behind the laughter, there may be tears,
In little gestures, profound healing appears,
A simple act of kindness, a beacon of light,
Can lift the weary, ignite hope's gentle flight.

The burdens we bear, they may not be shared,
But kindness, a balm, can show how we've
fared,
In this complex tapestry, woven with care,
Each thread connecting us, a reminder to bear.

So let us be kind, with hearts unassuming,
For in the depths of souls, understanding is
blooming,
A kind word, a gesture, a listening ear,
Can bring solace, soothe afflictions we fear.

For we all face battles, unseen to the eye,
A struggle, a longing, a silent goodbye,
And in this web of life, let compassion be sown,
For we know not what someone is going
through, unknown.

God is always there

God will always be there, loving you, being proud,
In the vast expanse of the universe, His grace endowed.
A majestic presence, infinite and ever true,
Embracing your soul, in all that you are and do.

No matter the storms that may rage and tear,
His love, a guiding light, will always be there.
Through trials and tribulations, He stands tall,
Whispering softly, His embrace will never fall.

In moments of doubt, when darkness surrounds,
His love, a beacon of hope, forever resounds.
With arms open wide, He welcomes you home,
A sanctuary of love, where you'll never be alone.

Unfathomable, His love knows no bounds,
Reaching across galaxies, without any bounds.
In every breath you take, His presence abides,
A constant reminder, even when tears subside.

Through the joys and sorrows, the highs and lows,
God's love remains steadfast, as the river flows.
He rejoices in your triumphs, in every victory,
His pride knows no limits, for you are His story.

His love, a tapestry woven with divine thread,
Each moment, a masterpiece, in which you're led.
With every step you take, He walks by your side,
Invisible, yet omnipresent, His love cannot hide.

So fear not, dear soul, for you are not alone,
God's love surrounds you, even when the winds have blown.
He will always be there, loving you, being proud,
In the vast expanse of the universe, His grace endowed.

Proud of you

In the depths of uncertainty, when shadows loom,
When doubt creeps in and casts its gloom,
Remember these words, my friend,
A beacon of strength, a light to infuse.

In case no one told yet, hear it from my heart,
I am proud of you, for your determined start,
A journey embarked upon, with courage anew,
You're forging ahead, and I am proud of you.

Keep going, my friend, with an unwavering stride,
In the face of adversity, let your spirit guide,
For dreams are the compass that leads us on,
Through valleys and peaks, until they are won.

Do not ever give up, when the path feels unclear,
When obstacles arise and doubt whispers near,
You have the strength within, like a warrior's fire,
Ignite your passion, let it take you higher.

Do not listen to the haters, their venomous words,
For they know not the battles, the dreams they've blurred,
Your worth is not measured by their shallow disdain,
Keep your focus intact, let their noise be in vain.

Do not let anyone stop you, from reaching your dream,
For your spirit is fierce, a force to redeem,
With unwavering faith, let your purpose shine through,
No matter the trials, I will always be proud of you.

Through the peaks and valleys, the twists and turns,
Your resilience will guide you, as the world learns,
That you are a force, a dreamer unbound,

And with every step taken, your victory is
crowned.

So, my friend, keep pushing ahead,
With passion and grace, let your dreams be fed,
In case no one has told you yet, let it be clear,
I am proud of you, and always will be near
No matter what happens I will always be here.

Birthday

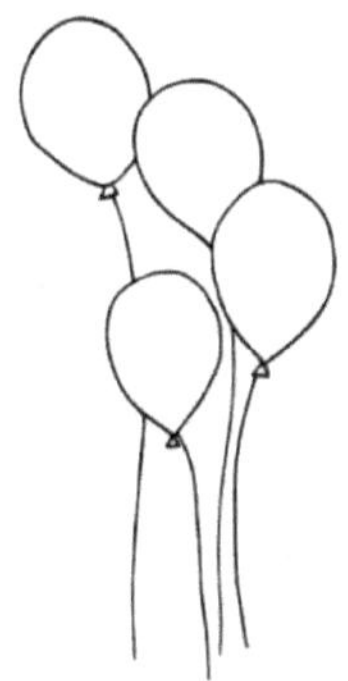

Birthday wishes
blow the candles out
as everyone sings around you
for today is the day we celebrate your birth
In this moment of joy,
time stands still,
as the flames dance and flicker,
illuminating your face with a warm glow.
Years have passed,
each one a chapter
in the story of your life,
etched on the pages of your heart.
From the first cry that echoed
through the walls of the delivery room,
to the first step you took,

tentative and wobbly, but bold.
You've grown, my dear,
like a tender bud blossoming
into a vibrant flower,
unfolding your petals to the world.
Through the laughter and tears,
the triumphs and defeats,
you've carried yourself with grace,
embracing both the light and the shadows.
Today, as the melodies of celebration
fill the air, let us pause
to acknowledge the beauty
that radiates from within you.
May the wishes whispered into the universe
find their way back to you,
like gentle whispers of love and hope,
carried on the wings of this special day.
May each candle you blow out
ignite the spark of dreams within you,
illuminating the path ahead,
where endless possibilities await.
For today, we gather,
to honor your existence,
to cherish the memories we've shared,
and to anticipate the adventures yet to come.
So, blow out the candles, my dear,
and let their glow guide you
through the next chapter of your journey,
with love, joy, and endless birthday wishes.

Thanksgiving

Thanksgiving, a day to gather in embrace,
With family and friends, our hearts efface.
In gratitude, we come together, hand in hand,
To celebrate the blessings on this fertile land.
The table adorned with abundance and delight,
A feast of love, a symphony of sheer delight.
Laughter fills the air, as stories intertwine,
Memories shared, like aged wine.
For on this day, we pause to truly see,
The gifts bestowed upon us, so abundantly.
From the simplest joys to life's grandest prize,
We count our blessings, as the soul sighs.
We raise our voices, say grace to God above,
For the shelter of His grace, the power of His love.
Grateful hearts we offer, in humble refrain,

For the blessings that surround us, like gentle rain.
Thanksgiving is not just a meal to be shared,
But a moment to cherish, a memory ensnared.
A time to reflect on what truly matters most,
And give thanks for the blessings that engross.
For family and friends, our hearts unite,
In this sacred moment, our spirits take flight.
We gather 'round the table, grateful and sincere,
Finding solace in the love that brings us near.
So let us celebrate this day of gratitude,
With open hearts and attitudes renewed.
May Thanksgiving remind us, year after year,
To cherish our blessings, hold them dear.
For in this celebration, we find solace and peace,
As gratitude within us continues to increase.
Thanksgiving, a day to treasure and adore,
A reminder of all that we've been given and more.

Heaven

In the realm of endless skies, where dreams reside,
Heaven whispers its secrets to each heart's side.

Yet, to everyone, its meaning takes a different shape,
A tapestry of hopes and beliefs, a soul's escape.
Peaceful children and adults dance in a world so fair,
Laughter echoes, filling the tranquil air.
No pain, no problems, just pure serenity,
A haven where worries and troubles cease to be.
Fields of flowers bloom, a vibrant tapestry,
Nature's palette entwined, a living symphony.
For some, Heaven is a garden, a sanctuary of grace,
Where beauty blossoms in every sacred space.
Belief, a choice, a path we tread,
Some embrace, while others may instead,
Question the existence of this ethereal place,
Yet, through diversity, we find solace, and embrace.
For God's forgiveness knows no bounds,
In every heart, redemption can be found.
As long as we open our lives to His divine light,
Heaven's door remains open, shining ever so bright.
So, let peace be our guide, and love be our creed,
In this vast tapestry of faith, we shall indeed
Discover the essence of Heaven, so pure and divine,
Welcoming all souls, regardless of their sign.

For Heaven, to everyone, is different, you see,
A reflection of their journey, their own decree.
Yet, in the end, it matters not what we believe,
For through grace and acceptance, we all shall
receive.

Love

Stop looking for your soulmate
Love will come to you when ready
In the vast expanse of time and fate
No need for urgency, no need to be steady
For love is a mysterious creature
A dance of chance, a delicate art
It weaves its threads, and it features
The meeting of souls, a cosmic part
You may have already met the love of your life
But not know it, not yet aware
In the hustle and bustle, the daily strife

Love may be hiding, playing unfair
Do not fret, do not despair
For love has its ways, its own design
When the timing is right, it will declare
Its presence, its magic, so divine
In moments unexpected, love will arrive
Like a gentle breeze, like a shooting star
It will awaken your heart, make it come alive
And in that instant, you'll know who you are
So stop searching, stop seeking
Let love find its way to you
In life's grand tapestry, it is speaking
In whispers, in serendipities so true
Embrace the journey, trust the flow
Love will come, when it's meant to be
Your soulmate is out there, this you must know
And when the time comes, love will set you free.

Together

In the depths of despair, a trembling soul
Falls into a deep dark abyss, losing control
Lost in the shadows, consumed by the night
Where hope fades away, swallowed by fright
But in this desolate realm, a glimmer appears
A hand reaching out, dispelling all fears
It extends from the void, offering solace and aid
Guiding the lost, lifting the spirit that's frayed
With hesitant steps, they reach for the light
Embracing the warmth, banishing the blight
The hand pulls them close, whispering words of might

"You are not alone, together we'll fight"
Through the darkness they walk, resolute and strong
Each step a triumph, each stride a new song
The path may be treacherous, strewn with doubt
But they press on, for there's no room for bowing out
In this journey, they find strength deep within
Unveiling the courage they thought they couldn't win
With every obstacle faced, they rise above
For in the face of adversity, they find love
Keep going, keep walking, the hand gently implores
Through the trials and tribulations, success is in store
For within the depths, a resilient soul is found
Ready to conquer, to rise from the ground
So let the abyss be a testament to their might
A reminder that darkness can always turn bright
Through the hand's unwavering support and embrace
They'll emerge triumphant, in this endless race.

Music

In melodies we find solace, a refuge from life's strife,
Where worries fade to shadows, and burdens take their flight.
For music holds the power, to heal our weary souls,
To transport us to realms, where tranquility unfolds.
Through symphonies and sonnets, our spirits are set free,
As notes dance on the airwaves, with graceful harmony.

They weave a tapestry of sound, that speaks without a word,
And in their gentle cadence, our troubles are unheard.
In each rhythmic pulse and beat, lies a soothing balm,
That eases troubled thoughts, like a tender healing psalm.
It whispers in our ears, with a voice so sweet and clear,
A melody that resonates, banishing all our fear.
From the gentle lullabies, that calm an anxious mind,
To the vibrant rhythms, that make our bodies unwind,
Music wraps around us, like a warm and loving embrace,
Guiding us to a place, where serenity finds its space.
In the symphony of instruments, we find our own refrain,
A chorus of emotions, that eases every pain.
The strings, they sing of longing, and the keys, they softly weep,
While the drums, they roar with passion, and the flute, it sings so deep.
So let the melodies wash over you, like a gentle summer rain,

Let the harmonies envelop you, and soothe away the strain.
For in the realm of music, problems find no place,
As it carries us to a realm, where tranquility finds its grace.
So when troubles weigh upon you, and stress begins to rise,
Let music be your solace, let it be your sweetest prize.
For in its gentle embrace, you'll find respite and release,
As music makes you forget about the problems you face.

Childhood memories

In the realm of childhood memories,
Where dollhouses danced in make-believe,
And laughter echoed through the trees,
I roamed with innocence, wild and free.
With nimble fingers, I crafted dreams,
Tiny furniture and miniature scenes,
Lost in a world of endless play,
Where time stood still, day after day.
Mud pies, a messy masterpiece,
With muddy hands, we found release,
Creating culinary wonders with glee,
Feasting on joy, so carefree.
My sister and friends, partners in crime,
Together we soared, like birds in rhyme,

Exploring the vastness of our imagination,
Building castles, without hesitation.
No worries, no stress, just pure delight,
As we chased the sun from morning to night,
Through secret hideouts and secret codes,
We conquered worlds, untamed and bold.
Oh, how I yearn to rewind the clock,
To frolic in childhood's magical stock,
To relish in those moments, long gone by,
When time was but a fleeting sigh.
But though I can't reclaim the past,
Those memories forever will last,
In the corners of my soul, they reside,
A treasure trove of joy, deep inside.
So, I'll hold onto those cherished days,
In dreams and whispers, my heart shall play,
For in the tapestry of my life's design,
Childhood's essence, forever intertwined.

Serene world

In a world where hatred does not reside,
Where innocent lives are not left to hide,
Responsibility dwells within each soul,
And pain and suffering no longer take their toll.
Oh, how I yearn for a place so serene,
Where the rainbow's colors forever gleam,
A glimmer of hope, a beacon so bright,
Guiding us towards a harmonious light.
Will this chaos cease, will peace prevail,
In a world where unity shall never fail?
I dream of a time when love conquers all,

And war's bitter echoes no longer enthrall.
No more cries of anguish, no more tears,
Only compassion that erases our fears,
In this utopia, kindness will reign,
And empathy shall heal every heart's pain.
Oh, how I long for that world to be,
Where nations embrace in unity,
A tapestry woven with threads of peace,
Where conflicts and divisions finally cease.
But until that day, we must strive and believe,
That change is possible, if we conceive,
That each step we take, each word we share,
Can bring us closer to a world so fair.
So let us hold on to the glimmer of hope,
And nurture the seeds of love we can sow,
For in our hands lies the power to create,
A world where harmony will resonate.

Friends

In this vast world, where souls wander,
Good friends are rare, a treasure to ponder.
Seeking hearts, longing for connections,
Yearning for bonds, built with affection.
They are the ones, who see through the veil,
Embracing your flaws, as if a fairytale.
Unveiling your essence, without any pretense,
Accepting you wholly, no need for defense.
Through ups and downs, they steadfastly stand,
With open arms, they extend a helping hand.
In the realm of acceptance, they reside,
A shelter of solace, where you can confide.
They listen intently, without judgment or scorn,
Each word you utter, lovingly adorned.

They hold your secrets, like precious gems,
Understanding your soul, beyond mere whims.
No need to wear masks, or pretend to be,
For they embrace your quirks, so lovingly.
You can be vulnerable, your true self revealed,
With good friends, your heart is truly healed.
Hold on tightly to these rare gems you've found,
For they are the ones who truly astound.
In a world that's ever-changing and unknown,
Good friends are the roots that help us grow.
So cherish them dearly, in your heart they reside,
A bond that transcends all space and time.
For good friends are rare, a treasure so true,
Hold on to them tightly, they'll always hold on to you.

Tennessee

In the small countryside of Tennessee,
Where dreams are born and set free,
There lies my vision, my cherished dream,
Of owning land, where hope shall gleam.
A place where children can laugh and play,
A haven that brightens their every day,
An all-inclusive daycare, my heart's desire,
Where love and acceptance shall never tire.
Amidst the rolling hills and fields so green,
Farm animals roam, a delightful scene,
Their gentle presence, a calming embrace,
As children learn the beauty of nature's grace.
Equine therapy, a realm of healing,
Where horses and children find a special feeling,

Together they'll grow, both strong and kind,
Unlocking potentials they never thought they'd find.
For those who doubted, who whispered disdain,
Saying I couldn't achieve, that I'd never gain,
I'll prove them wrong, with unwavering might,
Turning their doubts into sparks of light.
The path may be tough, with obstacles to face,
But determination shall guide my every pace,
With hard work and passion, I shall succeed,
In bringing my dream to life, fulfilling my need.
So, I'll carve my destiny in this land,
With love as my guide, I'll take a stand,
To create a haven, where dreams come alive,
Where children flourish, and hearts can thrive.
In the small countryside of Tennessee,
My dream shall blossom, for all to see,
A testament to resilience and belief,
That anything is possible, beyond grief.

Conquer the skies

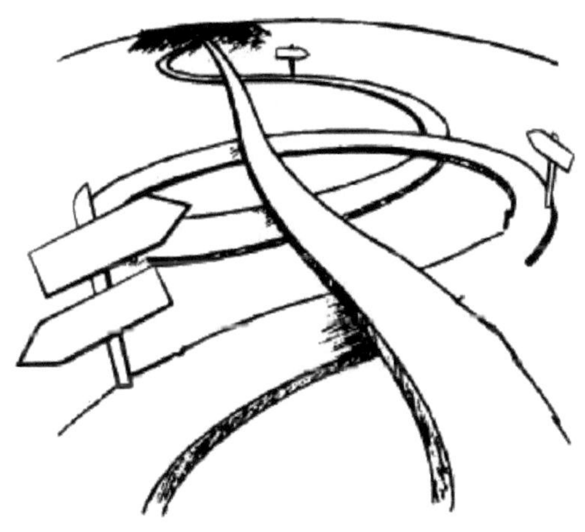

Leave toxic people behind,
When they keep putting you down,
Use it as motivation,
To help you succeed,
To prove them wrong.
You are allowed to let go,
Of people who cause you damage and pain,
For in their presence, you wither,
But in your absence, you bloom.
Keep looking up,
As the stars guide your way,
Soon your plans and wishes,
Shall come true, come what may.
For toxic souls may darken,

But they cannot extinguish your light,
Let their negativity be fuel,
To ignite your inner might.
In this vast universe,
You are the captain of your fate,
With each step forward,
You leave behind the weight.
So, shed the chains of toxicity,
Embrace your freedom, unbind,
For in the realm of self-discovery,
True serenity you shall find.
Leave toxic people behind,
For they hinder your growth,
Let their absence be a reminder,
Of the strength you've always known.
You are worthy, you are strong,
Unleash your spirit, let it soar,
With every leap, with every stride,
You forge a path worth fighting for.
So, let go of those who dim your light,
Surround yourself with love and cheer,
Believe in yourself, believe in your dreams,
Success is near, it's drawing near.
Leave toxic people behind,
And watch your spirit rise,
With determination as your guide,
You'll conquer the endless skies.

Rain

Rain tip-tapping at your windows,
A gentle rhythm, a melodic flow,
A symphony of droplets, a soothing sound,
Nature's tears, falling to the ground.
The gray clouds cover the vast expanse,
Blanketing the sky in a muted dance,
The world immersed in a watery haze,
As raindrops fall in a tranquil daze.
But fear not, for this storm shall pass,
The rain will cease, the clouds won't last,
For beyond the gray, a promise is made,

A vibrant rainbow will soon be displayed.
In hues of red, orange, yellow, and green,
A kaleidoscope of colors to be seen,
Arching gracefully across the sky,
A breathtaking sight that catches the eye.
So, hold on tight, endure the rain's embrace,
For soon the storm will leave no trace,
And as the clouds disperse, hope will grow,
With a radiant rainbow on full show.
Let the rain cleanse your troubles away,
Let it wash away the gloom and dismay,
Embrace the beauty that follows the storm,
For after the rain, a new day is born.
Rain tip-tapping at your windows,
It will soon be over, and a rainbow will show,
A reminder that storms don't last forever,
And even in darkness, there's always a sliver of
light to endeavor.

Pets

In the realm of pets, a joy untold,
From cats to dogs, birds to fish, behold!
They grace our lives with love unreserved,
A comfort in times when hearts feel perturbed.
With furry paws and wagging tails,
They chase away our worries, like gentle gales.
Their purrs and barks, a sweet symphony,
Melodies of solace, in perfect harmony.
Each creature unique, with its own charm,
From playful antics to feathers that disarm.
Their vibrant colors, a sight to behold,

In every hue, a story untold.
When sadness grips, or stress takes its toll,
They lend a paw, a wing, a fin, to console.
With tender eyes, they speak without words,
Their presence, a balm, like the songs of birds.
Oh, how they know, our deepest fears,
And cast away troubles, like forgotten tears.
They offer a love so pure and sincere,
A bond unbreakable, year after year.
Yet, in our flawed ways, we often forget,
The grace they bestow, we do not merit.
For in their eyes, we see no fault,
Just boundless affection, never to halt.
So let us cherish these pets we keep,
In our hearts, their love runs deep.
For they teach us lessons, a priceless treasure,
Of loyalty, forgiveness, and endless pleasure.
In the realm of pets, a blessing bestowed,
Through laughter and tears, their love has flowed.
A reminder to be kind, to love, to care,
For these precious beings, beyond compare.

Lost in a book

In the realm of reading, let us wander,
Where words entwine, and thoughts meander,
A sacred space, where dreams unfurl,
Where imagination paints its swirl.
In pages bound, we find escape,
From everyday, mundane landscape,
Where weary souls seek solace sweet,
In stories old, or tales complete.
Within the lines, a portal lies,

To realms unknown, yet recognized,
With every word, a journey starts,
A ticket to the world of arts.
Oh, reading, you're a passport rare,
Transporting minds beyond compare,
To foreign lands and distant shores,
To cultures rich, and so much more.
With eyes alight, we navigate,
Through ancient times, or futures great,
We walk beside heroes brave and true,
In worlds unseen, but felt anew.
Oh, reading, you're the key that frees,
Unlocking doors to fantasies,
Through poetry, we find release,
A language of the soul's inner peace.
In verse or prose, we find our way,
Through chapters long or poems, they say,
We wander freely, hearts unbound,
In literature's enchanted ground.
And time, it fades, as pages turn,
For hours slip, and clocks adjourn,
Within the realm of ink and thought,
A moment's pause, forever caught.
So, let us cherish your sacred art,
Oh, reading, you're a work of heart,
Where we get lost, and yet we find,
A piece of ourselves left behind.

Realm of Words

In the realm of words, where dreams take flight,
Where imagination dances, pure and bright,
With pen in hand, and a blank canvas vast,
I write, where my thoughts run wild and free, steadfast.
No rules to bind, no limits to confine,
Just endless possibilities, mine to define,
With each stroke of ink, a world unfolds,
Where stories are woven, and magic beholds.
In this realm of wonder, where fantasies reside,
I paint pictures with words, where dreams coincide,

Mountains soar high, touching heavens above,
While rivers of thoughts, flow with endless love.
Creatures of myth, they come alive,
With my words as wings, they fiercely thrive,
Unicorns gallop, and dragons breathe fire,
In this realm of mine, where desires never tire.
Where heroes arise, with valor untamed,
And heroines conquer, unafraid and unshamed,
They battle their demons, with courage
profound,
In this realm of words, where strength is found.
Through meadows of prose, I freely roam,
Exploring the depths of my mind, I call home,
Ideas intertwine, like vines in a maze,
In this world of letters, where I'm forever ablaze.
A poet's haven, where emotions collide,
Where love and heartbreak, side by side,
I pour my soul, with each word I inscribe,
In this realm of freedom, where feelings reside.
Writing, my dear friend, you set me free,
To wander, to wonder, to truly be me,
In the realm of my words, I'll forever remain,
Where imagination runs wild, with no restraint.

Books

Pages come alive,
Worlds unfold before my eyes,
Lost in tales I find.
Words paint landscapes grand,
Imagination takes flight,
Books, my passport true.
Mysteries untold,
Whispers from forgotten times,
Enchanted escape.
Minutes turn to hours,
Time's grip loosens its hold,
In pages I dwell.
Travel without cost,5kijthrough stories, I roam freely,
Exploring the unknown.
Lost in boundless tales,
Uncharted realms I explore,
Reading sets me free.

In a book's embrace,
I find solace and respite,
Lost, but never lost.

Magic in Nature

In nature's gentle embrace, I find solace,
Where peace whispers softly, a tender grace.
Sitting outside, basking in daylight's glow,
As birds orchestrate their melodious show.
Their sweet songs, like whispers in the breeze,
Lift my spirits high, put my heart at ease.
A symphony of chirps, a chorus so bright,
Filling the air with pure, untainted delight.
And as the sun sets, painting the sky with gold,
I linger outside, where stories unfold.
The crickets emerge, serenading the night,
Their harmonious tunes, a lullaby's delight.
In this tranquil moment, worries take flight,
Nature's soothing presence, a healing sight.
For once, the weight upon our weary souls,
Is lifted, as nature's embrace consoles.
No longer bound by the chains of our fears,
We're free to dream, to wipe away our tears.
The rhythm of nature, a melody profound,
In its gentle cadence, serenity is found.

Nature's tapestry, woven with such care,
Invites us to pause, to simply be aware.
To listen, to witness, the wonders untold,
And find inner peace, as nature unfolds.
So let us immerse ourselves in this embrace,
Discover the magic, that nature can trace.
For in its presence, worries shall depart,
And the tranquil symphony shall heal our hearts.

Christmas Morning

On Christmas morning, children running downstairs,
Eager to discover the gifts that Santa has shared.
Cookies left out for him, in the stillness of night,
Anticipation fills the air, a magical delight.
Laughter echoes through the halls, as they rush to your room,
Their voices gently wake you, chasing away the gloom.
Christmas time is here, as snowflakes softly descend,
A symphony of joy, a season without end.
Family and friends gather, their laughter fills the air,

Hearts united in merriment, a bond that's ever rare.
As you celebrate together, love and warmth embrace,
Christmas spirit shining bright, lighting up each face.
In the midst of winter's chill, a celebration so grand,
A reminder of the blessings, held tightly in our hands.
The magic of this season, in every joyful sound,
A chorus of gratitude, spreading all around.
So let us embrace this time, with open hearts and cheer,
For Christmas is a beacon, dispelling doubt and fear.
As snowflakes dance and twirl, we find solace in their grace,
A reminder of the beauty, in this enchanting place.
Christmas is coming, children running with glee,
Embracing the wonder, like waves upon the sea.
May this season be a reminder, of all that truly matters,
Love, laughter, and togetherness, shared with friends and family, forever and after.

Failure is a myth

Do not ever let
Doubt extinguish your fire
Dreams defy the dark
Believe in yourself
For within lies boundless strength
Failure is a myth
The naysayers scorn
But their words hold no power
Your spirit soars high
Reach for the heavens
Let your dreams guide your journey
Success will be yours
With determination
And unwavering resolve

You'll conquer the skies
In the face of doubt
Prove them wrong, let your light shine
Dreams, they know no bounds
So, dear dreamer, rise
Embrace the limitless sky
Your hopes, they will soar

Loved one

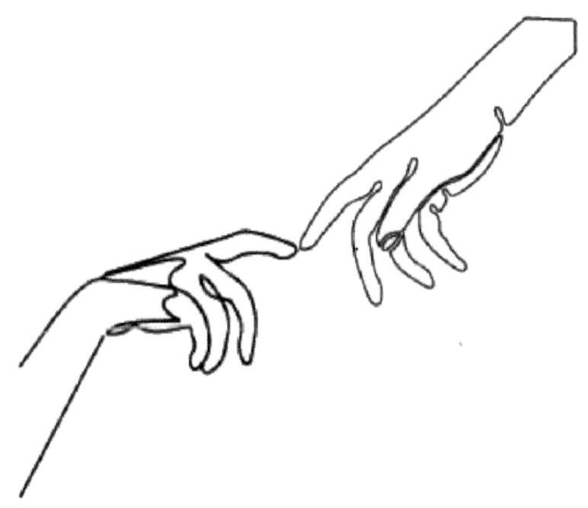

The wind you feel blowing in your hair is a loved one's kiss,
Caressing your cheeks with a gentle caress,
A whispered embrace, a presence unseen,
Guiding you through life's uncertain stream.
From above, they watch with tender care,
An angel in spirit, always aware,
Sending signs in the form of a lucky find,
A penny on the ground, a message designed.
Butterflies and birds, their colorful flight,

Symbols of joy, filling your sight,
They dance and they soar, in graceful array,
Reminding you that your loved one is near,
every day.
Their wings fluttering, a proud display,
Applauding your steps, along life's winding way,
For every milestone, every victory won,
They celebrate with you, their love brightly
shone.
So, embrace these signs, these whispers from
afar,
For in each one, you'll find a loving star,
A reminder that you're never alone,
With a cherished presence, forever known.
The wind, the penny, the butterflies' flight,
All gifts from above, a beacon of light,
Guiding your path, with love so profound,
Your loved one's spirit forever surrounds.
Let these signs be a comfort, a source of cheer,
A reminder that your loved one is always near,
In every moment, every step you take,
Their love and pride, a bond that won't break.

Dreams

Dreams do come true
keep trying
do not give up
In the depths of your soul
where dreams are born
a flicker of hope, a spark of desire
ignites the fire within.
With each step you take
towards the horizon of your dreams
you breathe life into your aspirations

and defy the boundaries of the ordinary.
The road may be winding
and the path may be steep
but with unwavering determination
even the impossible can be reached.
Through setbacks and struggles
you must persevere
for dreams do not unfold effortlessly
they require sweat, tears, and sacrifice.
When doubts cloud your vision
and failures cast shadows on your heart
remember, dreams do come true
for those who refuse to surrender.
So keep pushing forward
with passion as your guide
let your spirit soar, unburdened
and let the world witness your rise.
In this journey of fruition
where dreams are realized
let perseverance be your compass
and resilience of your trusted ally.
For dreams do come true
keep trying
do not give up.

Strength

Wipe those tears away, my dear,
Let not the sadness linger near,
For in your heart, love shall reside,
And hate's cruel whispers shall be defied.
The hurtful words they throw your way,
Hold no power over who you are today,
You are unique, special in your own right,
A beacon of strength, a guiding light.
Take a deep breath, let it all go,
Embrace the strength that lies within your soul,
With every smile, you defy their strife,
Showing the world the beauty of your life.
In the midst of the storm's fierce might,
You stand tall, ready to fight,
For no force can knock you down,
You rise again, wearing victory's crown.

So wipe those tears away, my friend,
Let love and joy be your guiding trend,
Embrace the power that lies within,
For in the face of darkness, you will always win.

Affirmations

In the realm of self-discovery, let us gather
To recite the affirmations that echo within,
Words that sing of strength and beauty,
Of love, unyielding, flowing from within.
Repeat after me, with conviction and grace,
"I am strong, a force that cannot be shaken,
Through trials and tribulations, I remain steadfast,
With resilience and courage, my spirit unbroken."

In the mirror's reflection, behold the truth,
A beauty that transcends the shallow gaze,
For it emanates from deep within the soul,
A radiance that time nor judgment can erase.
Allow these words to seep into your heart,
"I am loved, cherished by those who truly see,
For their affection, a balm that heals and mends,
A reminder of the love that resides in me."
No longer shall I seek validation, In the opinions
of those who fail to understand,

For my self-worth is not defined by others,
But by the strength and love I hold in my hand.
For they are the brushstrokes of a masterpiece,
Each flaw a testament to your uniqueness,
A symbol of the beauty that lies beneath.
So, let us stand united, in this sacred space,
Declaring our worth, just as we are,
With these affirmations, we claim our power,
And shine our light, like a guiding star.

Perfect

In the depths of my soul, a fire ignites,
A proclamation of my truest self,
With every breath, my spirit takes flight,
I embrace the essence, my inner wealth.
I am perfect, as I am, without doubt,
No need for validation or acclaim,
For my worth, I shall never live without,
In my own reflection, I stake my claim.
No family ties nor friendships can deter,
The strength that lies within, so brightly lit,
Their judgment, I refuse to let it occur,
My self-worth, I shall never permit.
With firm resolve, I rise above the fray,

Defying those who seek to bring me down,
Their words and actions hold no power, I say,
I stand tall, wearing my deserved crown.
For I am perfect, just the way I am,
No other's definition can confine,
I am the author of my life's grand plan,
In my uniqueness, I brightly shine.

Winter

In the winter's grip, the snow descends,
A season of holidays, where joy transcends.
White flakes dance from the sky above,
Covering all in a blanket of love.
The air is crisp, the cold bites our cheeks,
Yet our hearts are warmed, as laughter peaks.
Children in mittens, their faces aglow,
Creating memories in the purest snow.
Snowballs fly, with accuracy and aim,
Laughter echoes, a joyful refrain.

Carefree spirits, sliding down the hills,
Exhilaration flowing, as time stands still.
With every slide, worries dissolve,
In this winter wonderland, problems absolve.
The world outside fades into a dream,
As we embrace the magic, as it seems.
Footprints in the snow, a testament to play,
In this winter's haven, where worries sway.
We reclaim our innocence, pure and bright,
In this season of snow, our hearts ignite.
So let it snow, let it snow, let it fall,
For amidst the frost, we find our all.
Winter's embrace, a gift to us all,
A season of holidays, where souls enthrall.
In the snow, we find our freedom's crest,
A canvas of white, where dreams manifest.
So let us rejoice in this winter's glee,
As we revel in the beauty of being carefree.

Fall

Fall leaves changing color,
from green to orange, brown, and red,
a kaleidoscope of nature's art,
adorn the trees, a sight to behold.
Falling gently to the ground,
they create a mosaic, a tapestry,
that blankets the earth with rustic hues,
whispering tales of seasons gone by.
With rake in hand, I gather them up,
a chore turned into childish delight,

compelled by an urge to be young again,
to leap and dance amidst their crunchy embrace.
The air, crisp and cool, tingles my senses,
the aroma of autumn fills my lungs,
whispering promises of Halloween and
Thanksgiving,
as they approach with eager anticipation.
The scent of candy and sugary treats,
mingles with the aroma of roasted turkey,
while apple cider warms my hands,
and the sweet aroma of pumpkin pie tantalizes.
In this season of transformation,
nature paints a vibrant masterpiece,
and we find ourselves bewitched,
by the magic of fall's enchanting spell.

Spring

Spring animals come alive
Spring animals come out from hibernation
Birds come back from flying south
Raining all season long to help plants and flowers grow
Rain creating puddles for children to splish splash in
In the hushed winter slumber, nature's secret keep
Animals tucked away, in their cozy, dream-filled sleep
But as the sun stretches its golden rays, wide and bright

Spring awakens, casting off the cold, embracing the light
From deep within the earth, sprouts of green arise
Bursting forth with life, reaching for the skies
As the rain falls gently, a symphony in the air
Caressing each petal, each blade of grass, with care
The critters stir, emerging from their winter's rest
Stretching their legs, shaking off the chill in their chest
Bears lumber out, blinking at the newfound day
Deer gracefully prance, in search of a fresh green buffet
Birds wing their way back, from lands far away
Their melodies of joy, painting the skies with display
Chirping and singing, announcing their return
Their vibrant feathers shimmer, as they dance and yearn
The rain descends, a gentle rhythm from above
A gift from the heavens, nurturing with love
It kisses the earth, quenching its thirst with grace
Awakening the dormant seeds, with a tender embrace
Puddles form, like mirrors on the ground
Reflecting the world, upside down, profound
Children in their rain boots, with glee and cheer

Splish splashing, jumping, in laughter they
appear
Spring animals come alive, in this wondrous
season
Nature's grand orchestra, performing without
reason
Beneath the gentle rain, new life begins to sprout
A symphony of rebirth, in every breath and
shout
So let us celebrate, this bountiful time of year
When the world awakens, shedding winter's fear
As spring animals emerge, and birds take to the
sky
Let us revel in nature's beauty, with grateful
hearts, oh my!

Summer

Sun beating down on you
Perfect time for going for a swim in a pool or at the beach
Or simply running in the sprinklers
To cool off
Eating endless tubs of ice cream and cold drinks
Summer is way too hot for some
And the perfect amount of sun for others
The scorching rays embrace our skin
As we seek solace in the shimmering waves

Beneath the cerulean sky
Laughter echoes through the air
As children splash and play
Their faces gleaming with pure delight
Sand between our toes
Caresses our soles with tender touch
A gentle reminder of nature's gift
The salty breeze whispers secrets
As seagulls dance upon the shore
Their wings spread wide in joyful flight
We indulge in frozen treats
Melting sweetness upon our tongues
Quenching the thirst of summer's heat
Some seek refuge in shaded nooks
Seeking respite from the fiery orb above
Yet others bask in its warm embrace
For summer, the season of extremes,
Is a symphony of contrasts
A playground for both heat and cool
So let the sun beat down upon us
As we dive into the depths of blue
Or dance in the sprinklers' spray
For in this season of sun-kissed bliss
We find solace, joy, and release
In the perfect amount of summer sun.

Life's meaning

In quest of truth, we ponder and inquire,
What meaning lies within this mortal strife?
An enigma, elusive and afire,
What exactly is the meaning of life?
No single answer, universal and clear,
Yet wisdom whispers through the realms
unknown.
A tapestry of purpose, far and near,
In varied hues, its vibrant colors sown.
For each of us, a different path unfolds,

A tale unique, with chapters yet untold.
A canvas blank, awaiting artistry,
To find our essence, shape our destiny.
No doctrine shall confine or bind us tight,
It's open to interpretation, right?
In seeking truth, we journey deep within,
Unraveling the mysteries of the soul.
With open hearts, we learn to love and bring
Meaning to life, as we strive to be whole.
The purpose lies in the moments we create,
Connections forged, in kindness, love, and
grace.
In laughter shared, and tears we contemplate,
We find the meaning, in life's sacred space.
Let no one claim the answers as their own,
For life's true meaning is for each to find.
In solitude or company, we're shown
The purpose that ignites our hearts and minds.
So, as we wander on this cosmic ride,
Embrace the mystery, with eyes open wide.

Phones

In this age, where screens command our gaze,
A world ensnared by glowing digital haze,
Everyone glued to their phone, it seems,
Lost in a realm devoid of human dreams.
Gone are the days of heartfelt conversation,
Replaced by mindless scrolling and fixation,
No longer do we seek deep connection,
But settle for shallow, virtual affection.

Oh, how I yearn for the old-fashioned way,
Where face to face we'd converse and convey,
Meaningful words with genuine intention,
Creating bonds that defy mere invention.
I sit here, across from you, my dear,
Yet your attention remains glued to that sphere,
Can we return to a time less device-dependent,
And rediscover the art of being present?
Let's break free from this addictive trance,
Embrace the world beyond screens, take a chance,
Rekindle the joys of personal interaction,
And find solace in genuine human connection.
For in a world consumed by glowing distraction,
We must reclaim the power of real interaction,
Let's choose presence over virtual allure,
And rediscover the beauty of conversations pure.

Slumber

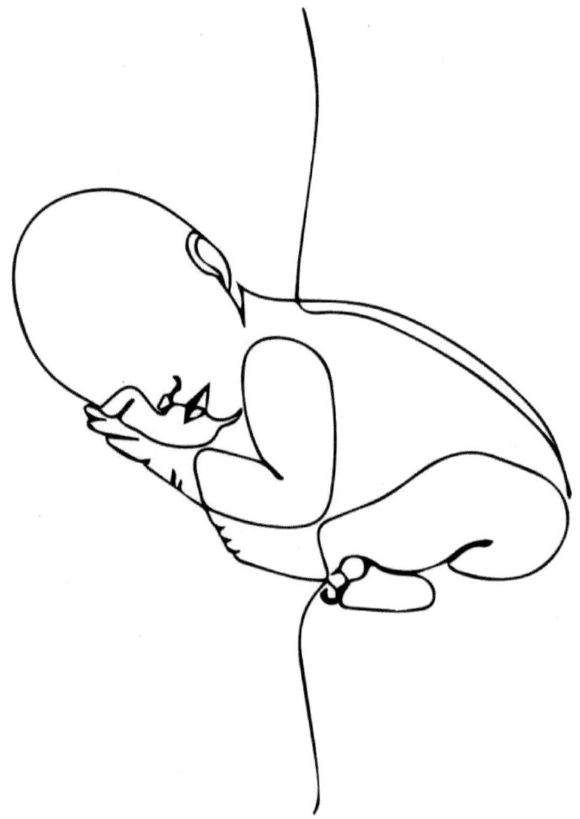

In the realm of dreams, where worries flee,
We find solace in the arms of sleep's decree.
A respite from chaos, a tranquil retreat,
Where time's relentless march finds swift defeat.

In slumber's embrace, troubles dissipate,
As consciousness surrenders to a blissful state.
A momentary respite from life's relentless grind,
Where burdens are lifted, leaving solace behind.
Oh, sweet sleep, the great equalizer of time,
Where seconds fly swiftly, like a fleeting rhyme.
In this ephemeral realm, hours turn to minutes,
As reality fades and the soul finds respite in it.
Here, in the realm of dreams, we find reprieve,
From the struggles and challenges we often perceive.
A sanctuary where worries cease to exist,
And the weight of the world gently subsists.
In the depths of darkness, we find our release,
Immersed in the stillness, finding inner peace.
Where everything disappears, fades into the night,
As we drift away, guided by slumber's light.
Sleep, oh gentle companion, grant us this plea,
To journey to realms where worries are set free.
For even if it's just a momentary escape,
In sleep's embrace, time's pace we reshape.
So let us surrender to this nocturnal retreat,
Where worries dissolve, and serenity meets.
In the arms of sleep, we find respite anew,
Oh, blessed slumber, we find solace in you.

Be kind

In this vast world, where shadows dance,
We cross paths with strangers, by mere chance.
Each soul harbors a secret storm,
A tale of battles fought, wounds forlorn.
Be kind, my friend, for you cannot see,
The battles fought behind their eyes, silently.
A smile, a word, a gentle touch,
Can mend the wounds that hurt so much.
For in this life, we all bear scars,
Some visible, some hidden within the stars.

A simple phrase, a tender deed,
Can sow the seeds of hope that someone needs.
In our encounters, let empathy guide,
For in another's shoes, we cannot hide.
Their journey, though unknown, deserves
respect,
A kind heart can heal, can reconnect.
A single act of kindness, so pure,
Can uplift spirits, help hearts endure.
For we are all travelers, on life's winding road,
And compassion, the fuel to lighten our load.
So be kind, my friend, for you never know,
The struggles faced, the sorrows they sow.
A gentle gesture, a compassionate view,
May change their world, transform it anew.
Remember, in this tapestry of life,
Weaving threads of kindness can conquer strife.
For the battles fought, the stories untold,
Deserve compassion, a love that's bold.
So let us be kind, with open hearts,
And paint a masterpiece, where kindness
imparts.
For in this world, where pain may reside,
A simple act of kindness can turn the tide.

Be Proud

Be proud of who you are today Covered in brilliance, not gray your struggles do not you, I admit But every moment of strife is worthwhile, in the end

Your darkest moments you still faced fear Yet you overcame, year after year From the ashes of who you once were A better you, you have become

So be proud of who you are today And strive to become a better you As the power to shape your life lies in your hands Believe in yourself and you can do anything, grand!

Nighttime

As nighttime falls upon us where most people are getting ready for bed,
The world takes on a cloak of shadows, a tapestry of secrets spread.

But in this realm of hushed whispers and starlit skies,
Some creatures stir, their nocturnal spirits rise.
While humans seek solace in dreams and slumber's embrace,
Animals emerge, eager to roam, in their own nocturnal chase.
Owls awaken from slumber, their keen eyes ablaze,
Silently soaring through the night, in mysterious ways.
The fox, agile and sly, tiptoes through the night,
Unfazed by the darkness, guided by lunar light.
Stealthy steps lead it to a realm unseen,
Where shadows dance and secrets convene.
Beneath the moon's gentle glow, the night creatures unite,
Invisible threads weaving their tales, hidden from sight.
The world spins on, oblivious to their nocturnal play,
A secret performance unfolding until the break of day.
And as you lie in slumber, oblivious to their plight,
The night's creatures traverse the darkness, their true delight.
For when you wake tomorrow, as dawn's first rays appear,

It's their time to retreat, as your world bursts into cheer.
So, remember, as nighttime falls upon us, casting its serene spell,
The creatures of the night awaken, their stories to tell.
Embrace the irony, the dance of lightness after dark,
For in this delicate balance, nature leaves its mark.

Darkness

Welcome darkness as an old friend,
For you have noticed that light always follows
after,
Even if it does not seem near.
Embrace the shadows that dance around,
In the corners of your weary mind,
For they hold secrets yet to be found.
In the depths of night's embrace,
Whispers of hope linger in the air,
Faint glimmers of stars, a celestial trace.
Fear not the obsidian veil that descends,
For within it lies the promise of dawn,

A new beginning, where all pain transcends.
When the world seems heavy and bleak,
And the weight of sorrow binds your soul,
Remember, solace is just a breath away, so to speak.
The darkest hour precedes the dawn's rise,
The blackest ink gives birth to vibrant hues,
And from the depths, life always defies.
So, welcome darkness with open arms,
For in its embrace, you shall find,
A strength that can weather any storm.
For light will come, as sure as the tide,
In its radiant glow, all shadows will wane,
And you shall triumph, side by side.
So, fear not the night, my dear friend,
For within its depths, a story unfolds,
A tale of resilience, until the very end.

Life

Life, a symphony of unpredictability,
A tapestry woven with threads of joy and sorrow,
A dance of light and darkness, intertwined,
Good, bad, and terrible, all in one embrace.
In this fragile existence, we seek solace,
A refuge in the beauty that surrounds us,
Yet, we must not turn a blind eye,
To the harsh realities that test our resilience.
Life's canvas painted with vibrant hues,

Each stroke revealing a hidden truth,
Amidst the chaos, we must persist,
For within the struggle, lies our strength.
Embrace the good, the moments that inspire,
The laughter, the love, that sets our hearts afire,
Let them ignite the flame within our souls,
To propel us forward when darkness takes its toll.
But do not dismiss the bad or the terrible,
For they too have lessons, painful yet invaluable,
In the depths of despair, seeds of resilience grow,
And courage blossoms where wounds once laid low.
Seek the silver lining, the ray of hope,
Amidst the storm, the chaos, learn to cope,
For within the cracks, resilience finds its way,
And in the face of adversity, we find our sway.
Life, an unpredictable journey, we navigate,
With open eyes, open hearts, and souls ablaze,
Embracing the good, acknowledging the bad,
Finding strength in the midst of all we've had.
So let us dance through life's unpredictable sway,
Embracing the light and the shadows each day,
For in the balance between good and bad,
We find the beauty in this life we've had.

Miracles

Miracles do happen, they whisper in the wind,
Whether you believe in God or another source,
In moments when hope seems thin, they gently begin.
They paint the sky with hues of gold and soft pastels,
As sunsets cascade like a cosmic dance,
Each stroke of beauty, a story it tells,
A reminder that miracles are not left to chance.
They bloom in the garden, amidst petals of grace,
Where fragile blossoms defy the darkest nights,

In their delicate embrace, they leave a trace,
Of resilience and strength, like celestial lights.
They echo in the laughter of a child's pure joy,
A symphony of innocence, untainted and bright,
In the sparkle of their eyes, miracles employ,
To bring warmth and solace, a beacon of light.
They whisper through the whispers of love's gentle kiss,
When hearts entwine in a dance of serenity,
In moments of connection, miracles persist,
Unfolding mysteries that defy our certainty.
They soar through the heavens, on wings of faith,
Guiding us through trials, when we lose our way,
In the depths of despair, they offer a wraith,
A lifeline of hope, to brighten the darkest day.
Miracles do happen, if we dare to believe,
In the unseen forces that govern this world,
For in the realm of wonder, our spirits receive,
The miracles that unfold, like banners unfurled.
So let us open our hearts, to the miracles of life,
Embrace the magic that surrounds us each day,
Whether from God or another source, in our strife,
Miracles do happen, in their own mysterious way.

Prayers

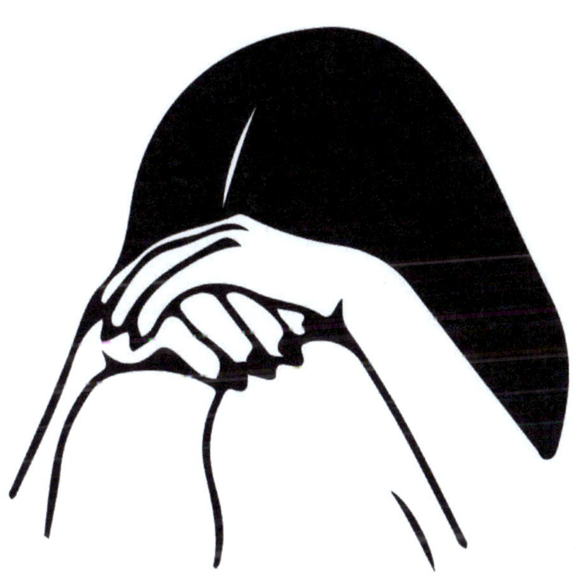

In the realm where faith resides,
Where prayers drift like whispered sighs,
There lies a truth, both old and wise,
That God is listening to our cries.
But patience, dear soul, is what we need,
For answers don't come with lightning speed.
For God, in His wisdom, has a plan,
To test our hearts and make us understand.
He grants our prayers, though time may pass,
In ways we may not always grasp.
Through trials and toils, He gently guides,

To show the answers that in us reside.
The path may seem obscure at first,
Yet blessings bloom when we put forth
The effort, the sweat, the labor, and strife,
To seek the answers in this earthly life.
For God is not distant, aloof, or cold,
But ever-present, His love untold.
He waits for us to recognize,
That prayers are answered in disguise.
So, fret not if the answers seem delayed,
For God is working in His own way.
He tests our faith, our souls He tends,
To show us the blessings that He sends.
In quiet whispers, amidst life's noise,
He speaks to us, His gentle voice.
And as we labor, as we strive,
We find the answers to prayers arrive.
So, have faith, dear one, and never fear,
For God is always, always near.
He listens, He answers, in His own time,
And molds our souls as we climb.
God's love is boundless, His mercy true,
He sees our struggles, our hearts He knew.
In every prayer, in every plea,
He's shaping us into what we're meant to be.
So, keep on praying, keep on believing,
For God is working, though not revealing.
And when the time is finally right,
The answers will come, bathed in His light.

Pennies

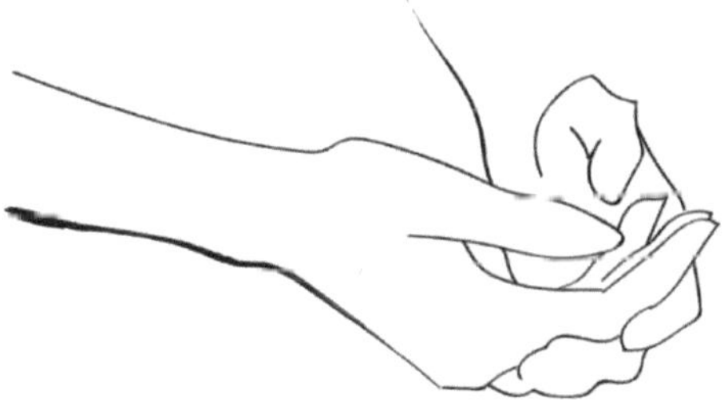

In realms unseen, where mysteries reside,
A notion whispers on the gentle breeze,
If fate allows, a penny shall preside,
A token found, a guardian to appease.
Have you ever heard, dear mortal soul,
This phrase that stirs the depths of wonder's sea?
When on a street, as footsteps take their toll,
A penny gleams, a symbol meant for thee.
An angel's touch, a sign from realms above,
To show they're near, though shrouded in
disguise,

A gentle nudge, a message born of love,
Ensuring safety through life's vast surmise.
Believe it or not, their presence intertwined,
In every step, their watchful eyes aligned.
So heed the whispers, let your heart be still,
For angels walk beside you, unseen grace.
Their wings unfurled, they guide with tender skill,
In every shadowed corner, every space.
They stand as sentinels, with steadfast might,
To shield your spirit from the world's cruel fate.
Through trials faced, they keep you in their sight,
Ensuring peace, a guardian innate.
Though doubt may cloud the path you choose to roam,
The angels' whispers guide you safely home.
So when a penny finds you on your way,
Take solace in the presence it implies.
An angel's touch, a blessing to convey,
A reminder of their love that never dies.
For in this world, where chaos oft prevails,
An angel's watchful eye shall never cease.
Embrace the truth, let faith and hope prevail,
And know their love shall bring you lasting peace.
In every penny found, a truth unfolds,
That angels watch over us, as life unfolds.

Church

In search of solace, find a church to call your own,
Where hearts are open, love unfettered, seeds of acceptance sown.
A sanctuary where judgment finds no fertile ground,
Where sexuality, disability, and race are not bound.
Seek a haven where love is not confined,
A place where lovers are embraced, hearts entwined
A church that celebrates love's diverse hues,

Where compassion and understanding are the only views.
Let the doors swing wide, inviting all to come,
No barriers erected, no souls left numb.
Find a second home, a refuge from life's storms,
Where warmth and understanding truly form.
For the broken and weary, the lost and confused,
A sanctuary where hearts and minds are fused.
Where differences unite, and prejudice is shed,
Embrace the beauty of diversity, in every thread.
Seek a church where open arms await,
Ready to embrace, to celebrate,
The unique tapestry of every soul,
Where love and acceptance make hearts whole.
In this sacred space, let prejudice fade,
The judgment's grip, no longer forbade.
For in the arms of this church, you'll find,
A love so pure, so gentle, so kind.
So seek that church, open and free,
A sanctuary that's boundless, like the sea.
Where love knows no bounds, and grace is given,
Find your second home, where souls are truly driven.

Sacred Pages

In the sacred pages of The Bible, verses intertwine,
A Bible's treasure, to keep us strong,
Stories of old, with wisdom so fine,
A common thread, where God's love belongs.
For God is present in each tale we read,
His watchful eyes, forever on our way,
Forgiveness offered, indeed a great deed,
His precious Son, on the cross did pay.
As long as we embrace Him in our hearts,
And humbly seek forgiveness for our flaws,
He'll pardon all our missteps and restarts,
For God knows well, we're bound to break His laws.
Imperfect souls, in need of divine grace,
In the Bible's verses, His love we trace.

To my dear friend:
Dedicated to one of my best friends- Anthony

To my dear friend,
Thank you for always being there for me,
Through the good times and the bad times,
For still continuing to be my friend through all this time.
I still remember the first time we met,
Playing games and laughing until our sides ached,

Even racing to complete the most mundane
tasks,
And oh, how I triumphed in that race!
If you're doubtful, my friend, a rematch is in
order,
But in truth, it matters not who wins or loses,
For friends like you are rare to find,
And I'm grateful for your presence in my life.
Thank you for sticking by me,
Through the twists and turns of life,
Even in the darkest of times,
You've been a beacon of light.
Your willingness to listen,
Without judgment or hesitation,
Has been a lifeline during my darkest days,
And for that, my dear friend, I'm forever
grateful.
May our friendship continue to blossom,
Growing stronger with each passing day,
Through every joy and every sorrow,
Thank you for always being one of my best
friends, always.

Oath to Coffee

Coffee, dear friend,
A vital elixir
Strength for weary souls.
One cup, then two, three,
Perhaps four to keep us fueled,
Caffeine's sweet embrace.
Sugar's gentle kiss,
Awakening our senses,
Cravings satisfied.
Hot or cold, we choose,
Indulging in our own way,
Coffee, our lifeline.
Without you, we're lost,
In a haze of drowsiness,
Grateful for your warmth.
Coffee, the lifeblood,
Guiding us through each new day,
Oath to your name.

Another world

Stars shining above us,
Their radiant light piercing through the night,
As we gaze into the vast expanse,
A tapestry of wonders, a celestial sight.
Maybe there is another galaxy,
Beyond our reach, beyond our grasp,
A realm of mystery, yet to be unveiled,
As we look into the night sky, we clasp.
Wondering if there is life,
In the depths of outer space,
Another world, perhaps still undiscovered,
A cosmic dance, an unknown embrace
The stars twinkle, a cosmic ballet,
Whispering secrets of distant realms,
Their luminous trails, a timeless legacy,
Guiding us through infinite helms.

We drift in awe, lost in contemplation,
Imagining worlds beyond our own,
Alien landscapes and uncharted constellations,
A universe waiting to be known.
But amidst our ponderings, we find solace,
In the beauty that surrounds us here,
For in each shining star, a story unfolds,
A reminder of the miracles we hold dear.
Stars shining above us,
Unveiling the wonders of the unknown,
As we marvel at the vastness of the sky,
We realize, our own world has seeds yet sown.

Parallel Universe

In the depths of our minds, curiosity stirs,
Do you ever wonder if alternate realms exist?
Where echoes of our lives are woven in a twist,
A universe where parallel paths persist.
Behind the looking glass, a secret may lie,
A gateway to a world unseen by the common eye,
Do we dare to venture, to seek and explore,
The realms beyond, where possibilities soar?
A reflection, a window, a mirror's embrace,

Could hold the key to a boundless new space,
Where versions of ourselves, different yet the
same,
Lead lives entwined, with a unique game.
Do they walk the same path, or choose a
divergent way?
Do they find love's embrace, or let it slip away?
Are they burdened by regrets, or filled with
endless bliss?
Do they mirror our choices, or surrender to the
abyss?
Perhaps in this alternate realm, we find what's
been lost,
A chance to rewrite the chapters, at a higher
cost,
To mend broken hearts, to heal wounds left
untamed,
To embrace second chances, where redemption's
flame is named.
But as we ponder this riddle, let us not forget,
That the world we inhabit holds secrets yet,
For there's magic in the moments, in the here
and now,
In the choices we make, and the love we allow.
So wonder, my friend, but let it not consume,
For life's tapestry unfolds, even in the simplest
room,
And though alternate universes may pique our
desire,

Let's cherish the one we have, and set our spirits afire.
For within our own hearts, a universe thrives,
With dreams to be chased, and passions to revive,
So let's navigate this journey, with hope as our guide,
In this world we call home, where our souls reside.

Making Friends

In the realm of connections, where hearts intertwine,
Making friends is not easy, as we journey through time.
Especially as we age, the world spinning fast,
We yearn for companionship, relationships that will last.
Gone are the days of seeking countless souls,
For now, we crave solace, a few who make us whole.

For in the depth of solitude, we come to realize,
It's not about quantity, but the quality that lies.
One or two, oh, what a treasure they shall be,
Those who truly understand, who set our spirits free.
No need for pretense, no masks to wear,
They accept us as we are, in our joys and despair.
They won't grow mad if we can't respond right away,
For they know life's demands have a role to play.
Patiently they wait, with understanding hearts,
Knowing that true friendship transcends distance and time's parts.
We can leave them alone for a year or two,
And when we return, it's as if time never flew.
They embrace us warmly, as if we just talked yesterday,
For in their eyes, our bond remains unswayed.
So cherish those friends, so rare and so true,
For they bring comfort and joy, all through and through.
In this journey of life, they're the stars in the night,
Guiding us, supporting us, with their love shining bright.
Making friends is not easy, as we grow old,
But those who stand by us, their worth can't be told.

So let us hold on to these priceless few,
For they are the ones who make life's colors anew.

Secrets

In whispers hushed, secrets do reside,
A treasure trove of thoughts, deep and profound.
Within our hearts, these mysteries confide,
A sacred bond, in trust they are bound.
Secrets are great things, hidden from all eyes,
Especially your own, kept close, unseen.

A realm where solitude and truth arise,
A realm where fragile souls find solace, keen.
For secrets are the emblems of trust,
A choice to share, a leap of faith untold.
When whispered words, in confidence adjust,
A sacred pact, a bond that will unfold.
So if a secret finds its way to you,
Take it as a sign, a trust brand new.

Young ones eager to learn

A young one so eager to learn,
seeing their growth with each turn,
A difference, I can sense,
for the knowledge I present,

I take pride in what I teach,
for the lives I help to reach,
From little ones to those up high,
As I teach, their minds can fly,

To watch them grow and understand,
To build a bridge and join one hand,
The difference made in their life,
Can't be measured with any knife,

From the moment they join the class,
To when one day, their life will pass,
The feeling of teaching making a difference,
Definitely a reason to fetch a person's existence.

A child’s hug

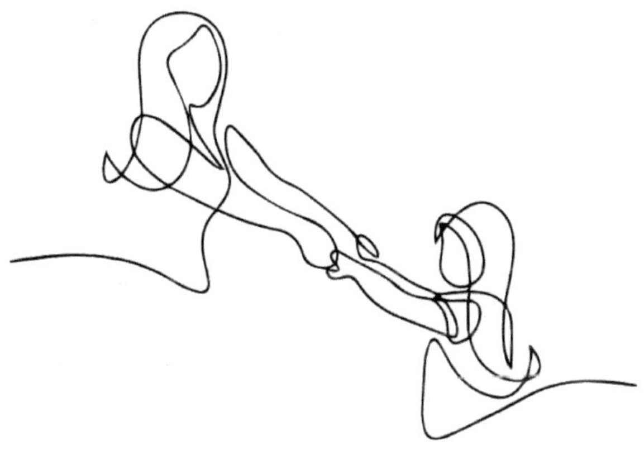

A child's embrace, oh so divine,
Wipes away each worry of ours,
Their playful antics bring us cheer,
And chase our sorrows far from near.
With every squeeze of their little arms,
Our heart is filled with joyous charms,
Their giggles and smiles erase our fears,
And leave us feeling calm and clear.
Children possess a special grace,
That knows just when to give a gentle trace,
Of love and comfort in their hugs,
And make our heart sing like a bug.
They sense our sorrows deep inside,
And offer solace with a smile and stride,
For they know that sometimes we all need,

To feel loved and secure in our deeds.
So here we will stay in this childlike state,
Where cares and woes are but a distant fate,
For in their loving arms we find our peace,
And our heart is forever released.

Still Hope Remains

Spark of hope remains still
In darkness that can seem to fill
War raging on, bills to pay
Mysteries still to be unfurled

Search for light further on
Rivers and valleys in between
End of the war ever near
Peace to find, what is to be seen

Hearts so heavy with unresolved pain
Still love remains, promises untold
Look deep may you find the joy inside
Of this immense life to behold

Sun rises ever anew
Peaceably, standing and tall
Shining ever brightly forward
Light at the end of tunnel awaits still

9 789358 316179

Printed by Libri Plureos GmbH in Hamburg,
Germany